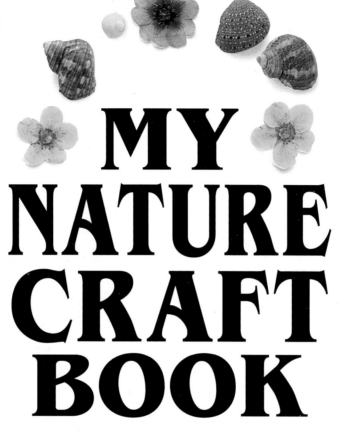

MY
NATURE
CRAFT
BOOK

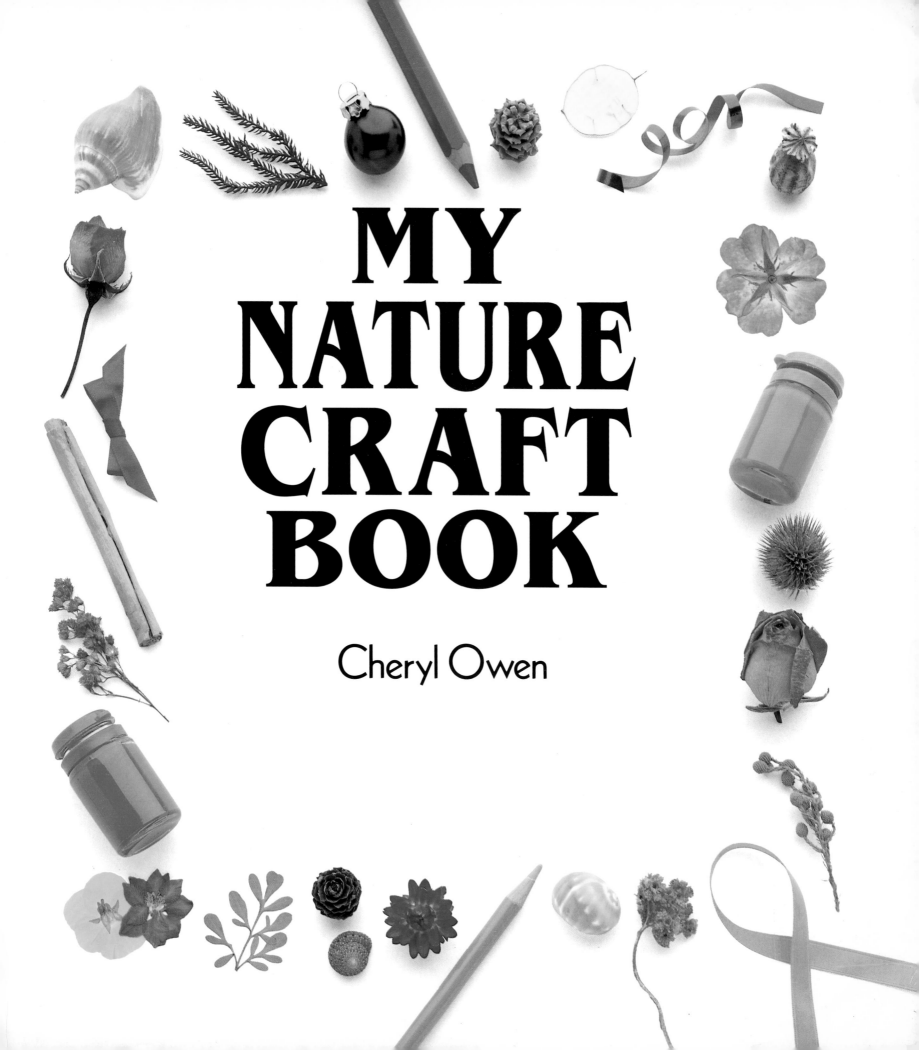

MY NATURE CRAFT BOOK

Cheryl Owen

A SALAMANDER BOOK

This edition produced in 2000
for Books Are Fun Ltd,
Fairfield, IA 52556, USA

© Salamander Books Ltd., 1993
129-137 York Way,
London N7 9LG,
England.

CREDITS

Managing editor: Veronica Ross
Art director: Rachael Stone
Photographer: Jonathan Pollock
Assistant photographer: Peter Cassidy
Additional designs by: Alan Dart and Caroline Green
Editor: Coral Walker
Designer: Anita Ruddell
Illustrator: Stan North
Character illustrator: Jo Gapper
Diagram artist: Malcolm Porter
Typeset by: Ian Palmer
Colour separation by: P & W Graphics, Pte., Singapore
Printed in Italy by STIGE Turin

Special thanks to Judy Taylor for her
contributions to this book.

CONTENTS

INTRODUCTION

With a growing awareness of the environment, many people have become more interested in their natural surroundings. *My Nature Craft Book* shows you how to create a wide selection of pretty and practical objects from things you can collect from your garden, the beach or a countryside walk. Learn how to print with a potato, to make a collage from seeds or a cute hedgehog from a teasel.

BEFORE YOU BEGIN

- Check with an adult before beginning any project; you might need some help.
- Read the instructions before you begin.
- Gather together everything you need first.
- Cover the work surface with an old cloth or newspaper.
- Protect your clothes with an apron or wear old clothes.

WHEN YOU HAVE FINISHED

- Put back the tops on glue and pens, wash paintbrushes and your hands.
- Tidy everything away. Store pens, paints, glue etc in old ice-cream containers or biscuit tins.

MATERIALS AND EQUIPMENT

When out on walks or on the beach, look out for things you can collect and use later: shells, stones, old driftwood, or fallen bark and cones from trees. Do not pick wild flowers without first asking an adult. Although there are some wild flowers which are plentiful on wasteland or in the hedgerows, many types are now threatened with extinction. Ask if there are any plants in the garden that you could pick to press or dry.

Also look around the home or garden shed for things to recycle: string, old boxes or scraps of leftover fabric. Remember to save cereal boxes, as they are a great source of cardboard. Tubes from kitchen or toilet paper rolls make great napkin rings, while dried herbs past their best are perfect for bath sachets.

SAFETY FIRST!

You will be able to make most of the projects in this book yourself. However, some of the designs use a sharp knife or an oven, and these projects have been marked with a SAFETY TIP. Do use common sense when using anything sharp or hot and ask an adult for help.

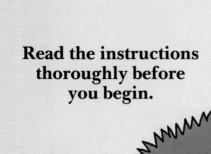

Read the instructions thoroughly before you begin.

USING PATTERNS

At the back of the book you will find the patterns you will need for some of the projects. Using a pencil, trace the pattern you need. If you are making a project with fabric, cut the pattern out and pin it on to the fabric. Cut out the shape. If you want to cut the pattern out of card, turn your tracing over and rub firmly over the pattern outline with a pencil. The pattern will transfer on to the card. Cut out this shape.

Once you have gained confidence making some of the projects, go on to adapt the ideas to create your own designs. If you enjoy drawing, try making up your own patterns freehand.

GROWN-UPS TAKE NOTE

Every project in *My Nature Craft Book* has been designed with simplicity, yet effectiveness, in mind. However, occasionally, sharp scissors or an oven will be needed. Your involvement will depend on the age and ability of the child, but we do recommend that you read through each project before it is undertaken.

And please remember these basic rules of safety:

- Never leave scissors open or lying around where smaller children can reach them.

- Always stick needles and pins into a pin cushion or a scrap of cloth when you are not using them.

- Never use an oven or a sharp knife without the help or supervision of an adult.

Never use an oven or a sharp knife without the help of an adult.

Some wild flowers are scarce. Check with an adult before you pick any.

YOU WILL NEED
Paper
Poster paints
Paintbrush
Leaves
Wax crayons
Narrow ribbon
All-purpose glue

Next time you are out on a walk, collect lots of different shaped leaves and practise making your own leaf print wrapping paper. Use the paper and the matching tags to make your presents look really original.

1 To make a print, carefully paint one side of a leaf with poster paint.

2 Lay the leaf face down on to a sheet of paper. Press the leaf down firmly with your fist. Remove the leaf and repeat to make another print. Once the printed leaves are dry you can wrap your present.

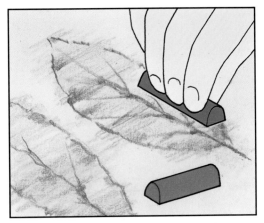

3 To make a gift tag, place a leaf under a sheet of paper. Rub a wax crayon over the paper until you see the leaf image appear. Cut out the leaf shape.

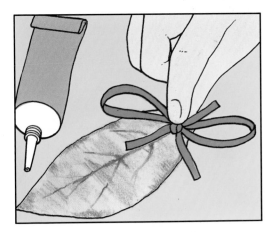

4 To finish, tie a ribbon bow and glue this to the tag. Write your message on the back of the tag and stick it to the wrapped present.

SUMMER HATS

Miniature straw hats look stunning when they are decorated with tiny bunches of dried flowers and ribbons. Try decorating a whole range of different sized hats and hang them on your bedroom wall.

1 Carefully glue a length of lace under the brim of a straw hat. Make sure that the decorative edge faces outwards.

2 Tie tiny bunches of dried flowers together with cotton thread. Arrange them around the crown of the hat.

3 Glue the flowers in place. You can glue on a single bunch or cover the whole brim of the hat with flowers.

4 To finish, tie narrow ribbon into a bow and glue it to the hat. Trim the ends of the ribbon.

PRESSED FLOWER CARDS

Pick flowers and leaves during the summer and press them to use as decorations for cards, gift tags and pictures. Flat daisy shapes press well, as do grasses, leaves and ferns.

1 Place the flowers and leaves on blotting paper. Fold the sheet over to cover them and press the flowers between the pages of a heavy book or in a flower press.

2 After a few weeks, carefully remove the flowers and leaves. Cut a rectangle of coloured card and fold it in half to make a greetings card.

3 Arrange the flowers and leaves in a pretty design on the front of the card.

YOU WILL NEED
Assorted flowers and leaves
Blotting paper
All-purpose glue
Heavy book or flower press
Coloured card
Scissors
Clear sticky-backed
  plastic

4 Carefully glue all the pieces to the card. You can cover the cards with clear sticky-backed plastic to protect the flowers from being damaged.

COCKATIEL COLLAGE

Pressed flowers and silvery honesty seed heads work well together to make colourful collages. Follow the instructions here to make this exotic cockatiel, or try drawing your own designs.

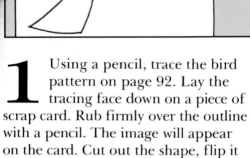

1 Using a pencil, trace the bird pattern on page 92. Lay the tracing face down on a piece of scrap card. Rub firmly over the outline with a pencil. The image will appear on the card. Cut out the shape, flip it over and position on the coloured card. Draw around the bird pattern.

2 Glue long leaves on to the cockatiel's tail. Lay pieces of honesty on the body, overlapping each one. Glue these in place. Add some long leaves as wings.

3 For the beak, glue on a small leaf and for the eye use the centre of a small flower. Glue on the stick to look like a perch and then glue on two little leaves as feet.

4 Make the famous crest on the cockatiel's head from yellow and white petals. Complete the picture by glueing small groups of leaves in two corners of the card.

YOU WILL NEED
Honesty or money plant
Pressed yellow and white petals
Other pressed small flowers
   and leaves
Small stick
Coloured card
Scrap card
All-purpose glue
Tracing paper
   and pencil

ANIMAL SEED PICTURES

These animal pictures are made from seeds and grasses. Here are instructions to make the squirrel, but the badger is made in the same way. You can also try drawing your own animal shapes to make a set of woodland collages.

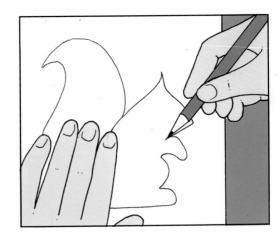

1 Using a pencil, trace the animal patterns on page 93. Lay the tracings face down on to scrap card. Rub firmly over the outlines with a pencil. The patterns will appear on the card. Cut out the shapes, flip them over and position on the green card. Draw around the patterns.

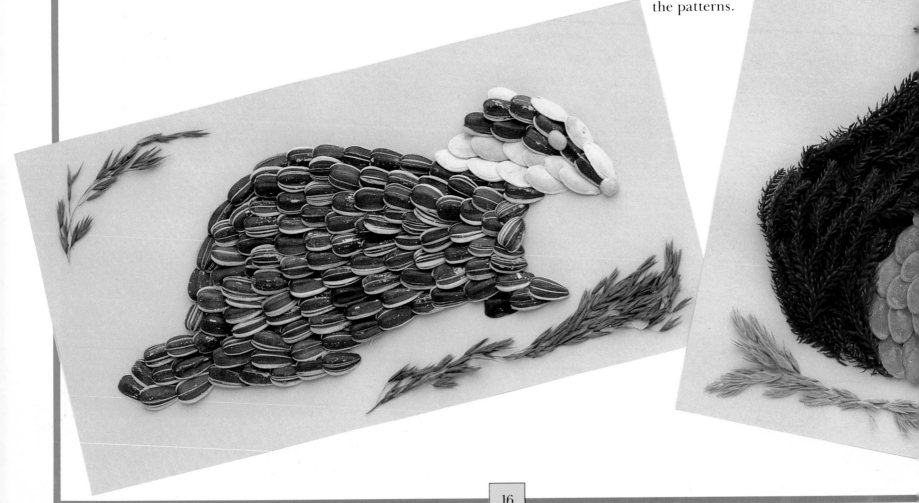

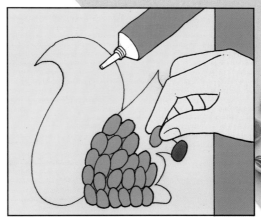

2 To make the squirrel, colour pumpkin seeds bright orange using a felt-tip pen. Break a hazelnut in half and glue it to the squirrel's paw.

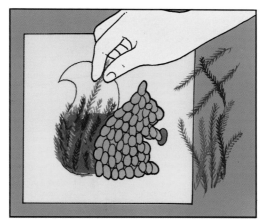

3 Overlap the seeds within the body shape and glue them in place. Stick a split pea on the face as an eye.

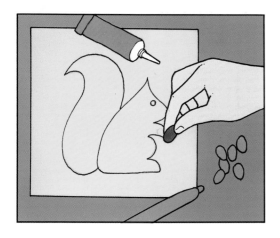

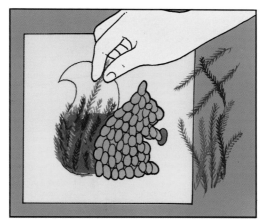

4 Glue red-coloured grasses to the squirrel's tail and other coloured grasses along the edges of the card.

YOU WILL NEED
Green card
Scrap card
Tracing paper and pencil
Sunflower and
   pumpkin seeds
A few split peas
Hazelnut
Coloured grasses
Orange felt-tip pen
All-purpose glue

LEAF LADY

Gather together a collection of autumn leaves and grasses from your garden and make this pretty collage. The leaf lady would make a perfect gift for a friend with an autumn birthday.

1 Using a pencil, trace the pattern on page 94. Turn the tracing over and lay it on to a sheet of firm paper. Rub firmly over the outline with a pencil. The leaf lady pattern will appear on the paper. Use colouring pencils to add the face details.

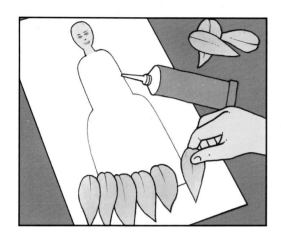

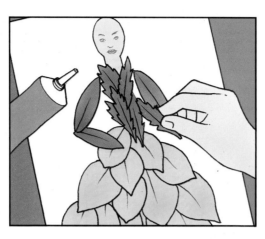

3 Use smaller, different coloured leaves for the bodice, and long thin leaves for the arms. Glue these in place carefully.

2 Use the largest leaves to make the leaf lady's skirt. Start at the hem and work upwards. Glue the tips of the leaves in place.

4 Finally, glue on some rat's tail statice for hair and put some leaves or ears of wheat in the leaf lady's arms.

YOU WILL NEED
Tracing paper
Pencil
Firm paper
Colouring pencils
Leaves and grasses
Rat's tail statice
All-purpose glue

STRING PRINTS

Use rope, string or other natural materials, such as bark, to make all sorts of interesting patterns with block prints. We have used string blocks to decorate table mats, a scarf and some notepaper, but you can print almost anything.

YOU WILL NEED
Thick cardboard
All-purpose glue
String, or other natural material
Acrylic paints
Paper or fabric to print
Scissors

1 To make a block, cut a piece of thick cardboard 3cm x 7.5cm (1½in x 3in).

2 Take a short length of string and coil it into an interesting shape, glueing it to the block as you work. Leave it to dry.

3 Dilute the paint with a little water and pour into a shallow dish. Dip the string block into the paint.

4 Shake off any excess paint and press the string block firmly on to the fabric or paper to make a print. Do not use too much paint or the pattern and texture of the string will be lost.

LAVENDER BAGS

Make these delightful scented bags from scraps of pink, blue or lavender coloured fabric filled with sweet-smelling lavender. Store the bags among your clothes to keep them smelling fresh.

1 Using pinking shears, cut out a rectangle of fabric roughly 18cm x 13cm (7in x 5½in).

YOU WILL NEED
Scraps of fabric
Pinking shears
Needle and thread
Dried lavender
Ribbon

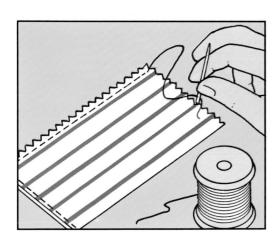

2 Fold the rectangle in half widthways so that the right side of the fabric is facing in. Sew along the bottom edge and the side edge, as shown.

3 Turn the bag the right way out and fill with a few handfuls of dried lavender.

4 To finish, tie a length of ribbon in a tight bow around the neck of the bag.

FRUIT POMANDERS

Smelling lightly of citrus and cloves, these fruit pomanders look especially pretty in the kitchen or bedroom, hanging from bright, cheerful ribbons.

YOU WILL NEED
Oranges and lemons
2.5cm (1in) wide ribbon
Cloves

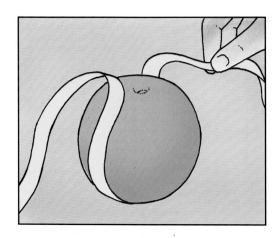

1 Fold a length of ribbon in half lengthways. Place the fruit on the ribbon and bring the two ends of the ribbon up around the fruit.

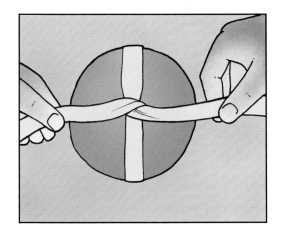

2 Where the ribbon meets at the top of the fruit, twist the two lengths of ribbon together, as shown. Take the ribbon back around the fruit and tie in a bow.

3 If you prefer, wrap the ribbon around the fruit just once. Tie a bow at the top and trim the ends of the ribbon neatly.

4 Now decorate the fruit with cloves. Push them into the skin of the fruit, either in a pattern, or covering the surface completely.

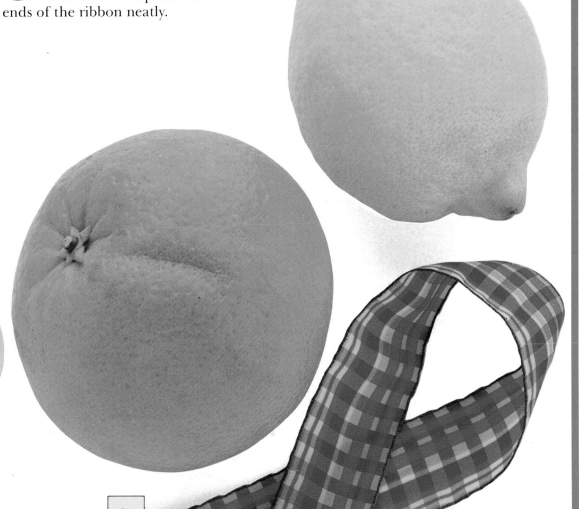

PAINTED STONES

Painted stones make pretty decorations and great holiday souvenirs. Next time you are at the beach collect some smooth stones to decorate when you get home.

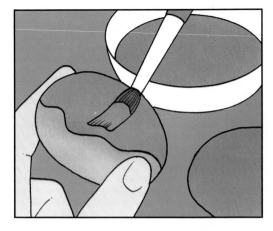

1 Wash the stones and leave to dry overnight. Paint on the blue background colour.

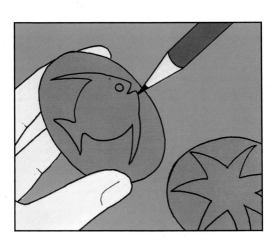

2 Draw a rough design on to a piece of paper. When you are happy with your picture, draw the outline on to the stone.

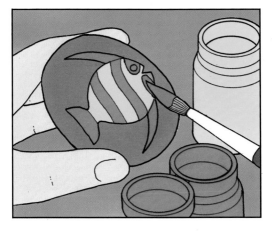

3 Following the outline of your design, carefully fill in the details with paint. Leave the completed stones to dry.

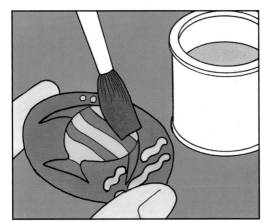

4 To keep your painted stones looking fresh and bright, coat your design with craft varnish.

YOU WILL NEED
Smooth stones
Poster paints
Scrap paper
Paintbrush
Pencil
Craft varnish

FANTASY TREES

These weird and wonderful trees 'grow' from poster paints. The natural looking designs can make really unusual cards, pictures and gift tags. Follow the instructions here, or try creating your own original designs.

1 Using the natural sponge, dampen both sides of the cartridge paper with water. Stick the paper on to a flat surface with gummed paper tape. This stops the paper from curling when wet. Smooth out any creases with the sponge.

2 When the paper is dry, dampen the sponge and dip it into watery blue-green paint. Dab the sponge over the paper to create the background.

YOU WILL NEED
Cartridge paper
Gummed paper tape
Poster paints,
    diluted with water
Small natural sponge
Eye-dropper
Drinking straw

3 Using an eye-dropper, carefully drop runny black or brown paint along the bottom of the paper.

4 Blow hard down a drinking straw while the paint is still wet to make the trees grow.

TEDDY BEAR CANDLE HOLDERS

These cute teddy bear candle holders are perfect for any birthday party. They are made from salt-dough, which can be made from basic ingredients in the kitchen cupboard. The ingredients here make one teddy bear.

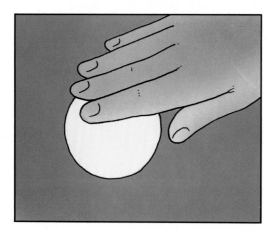

1 Mix the flour, salt and water together to make a ball of dough. Roll some of the dough into a ball about 4cm (1¾in) in diameter for the body. Squash the ball into an oval shape.

2 Roll a little more dough into a smaller ball for the head. Push the head on to the body. To make the ears and the muzzle, roll out two more balls of dough and cut them in half to create four semi-circles.

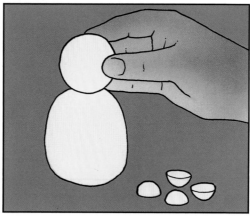

3 For the ears, press two of the semi-circles to either side of the head. The muzzle is made from one semi-circle, pushed on to the teddy's face. Use cloves for the nose and eyes, and draw a smile on to the face with a pin.

YOU WILL NEED
4 tablespoons plain flour
2 tablespoons salt
2 tablespoons water
3 cloves
Pin
Birthday cake candle
Poster paints
Paintbrush
Craft varnish

4 To make the arms, roll the dough into two sausage shapes and press these on to the sides of the body. Make a small dough bow and press this to the side of teddy's neck.

5 Take the candle and make a hole in the top of the bear's head. Remove the candle and ask an adult to help you bake the teddy in a cool oven at 110°C/250°F/Gas mark ½ for six hours. Paint and varnish the bear when cool.

SAFETY TIP: *Make sure an adult helps you when using the oven.*

MRS TEASEL HEDGEHOG

Collect some teasels growing wild in the countryside, and use them to make this cute Mrs Hedgehog. She is perfect as a gift, or you could make several to sell at a fund raising event or school fair.

1 To make the dress, cut the fabric into a rectangle 28cm x 11cm (11in x 4¼in). Sew ribbon and lace along the long bottom edge. Fold the fabric in half, right sides together, and sew along the short edge. Sew a running stitch along the upper edge and gather up the fabric.

YOU WILL NEED
Fabric scraps
Ribbon and lace edging
One large and one
  small teasel
Tracing paper
  and pencil
Pins and scissors
3 cloves
Beige felt and cotton wool
Dried flowers
Needle and thread
All-purpose glue

2 Slip the dress over the big teasel and glue it to the top. Glue a small teasel on top of this for the head. Glue on cloves for the eyes and nose.

3 To make the bonnet, cut a circle from fabric 14cm (5½in) in diameter. Sew lace around the edge of the circle. Sew a running stitch around the circle, 2cm (¾in) from the rim. Gather up the thread to form the bonnet. Put the bonnet on the head.

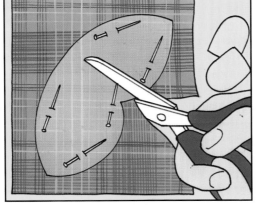

4 Using a pencil, trace the sleeve and paw patterns on page 95 and cut them out. Pin the sleeve pattern on to the fabric and the paw pattern on to the felt. Cut out two sleeves and two paws.

5 Fold the sleeves in half, right sides facing, and sew along the seam. Turn the sleeves right side out, and sew lace around the lower edge. Fill the sleeves with cotton wool. Place the paw in the sleeve. Gather up the sleeve around the paw and sew the fabric to the paw to secure. Glue the sleeves to the body. Glue a posy of dried flowers to the paws.

EASTER EGG TREE

This special Easter egg tree is fun and easy to make, and looks very cheerful when the eggshell baskets are filled with brightly-coloured flowers on Easter day. As a treat, fill the eggshells with miniature chocolate eggs instead.

YOU WILL NEED
Flower pot
Crêpe paper
All-purpose glue
Branch
Soil and moss
Blunt knife
Eggs
Ribbon
Fresh flowers

34

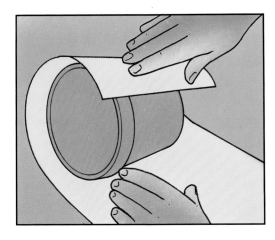

1 Cover a medium-sized flower pot with crêpe paper. Carefully glue the paper in place inside the pot and underneath.

2 Fill the pot with soil and plant into it a small branch to make the tree. Place moss on top of the soil, around the 'trunk' of the tree.

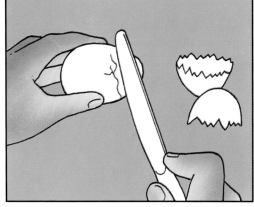

3 Using a blunt knife, gently tap around the centre of the eggs to crack them. Collect the yolks and whites of the eggs in a bowl (these can be used later for cooking), and leave the shells to dry.

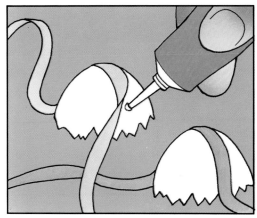

4 Glue a length of narrow ribbon around the eggshells as shown. Tie in a bow around a 'branch' on your tree.

5 To decorate, pour a little water into the eggshells and carefully add a few small flowers.

PRETTY GIFT TAGS

Pressing flowers is an easy and enjoyable project. On page 12, we show you how to do this. Here, we have used the flowers to make beautiful gift tags to add a special touch to a plainly-wrapped gift.

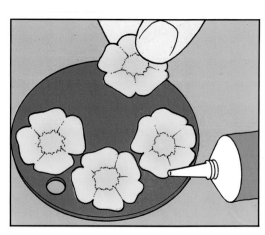

2 Arrange pressed flowers on to the gift tags. Glue the flowers in place.

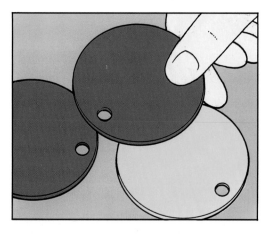

1 Cut circles and ovals from coloured card and punch a hole in the top.

YOU WILL NEED

Pressed flowers
Coloured card
Ribbon
Hole punch
All-purpose glue

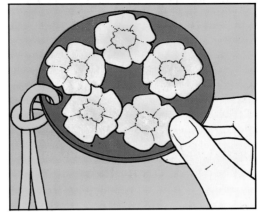

3 Thread narrow ribbon through the hole in the tags and tie it in a small knot.

4 Make some tags a little different by adding a small bow. To do this, make a few little bows from ribbon and glue them to the top of the tag.

HAIRY EGG HEADS

Here's a novel way to grow cress! Save the shells from eggs which have been used for baking to make these funny hairy egg heads. When the cress has grown, mix it with chopped eggs to make a delicious sandwich filling.

YOU WILL NEED
Empty eggshells.
Cress seeds
Cotton wool
Felt-tip pens
Egg box

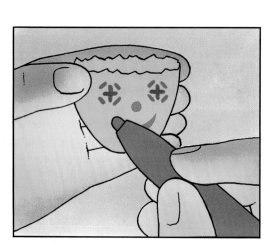

1 Wash and dry the eggshells. Draw a funny or scary face on each one with felt-tip pens.

2 Dampen some cotton wool with a little water and gently press it into the eggshells.

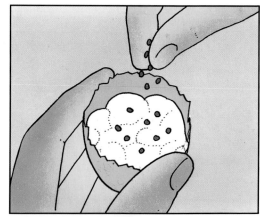

3 Carefully sprinkle a few of the cress seeds on to the cotton wool.

4 Stand the egg heads on a sunny window ledge in an egg box. Make sure that the cotton wool does not dry out. After a few days the seeds will sprout and grow 'hair'!

DRIED FLOWER GIFTWRAP

Simple dried flowers can transform a plainly-wrapped gift. Use grasses and flowers you have gathered and dried yourself or buy them from a local florist or market stall.

1 Wrap your presents neatly with shiny giftwrap, or place them in a pretty giftbag.

2 For a large square or rectangular present, arrange the dried flowers on top. When you are happy with the design, glue the flowers in position.

3 To decorate a small gift, wrap narrow ribbon around it, and slip a tiny spray of dried flowers under the ribbon.

4 For the giftbag, gather together a small bunch of dried flowers and tie them together with a ribbon. Finish with a bow and glue the posy to the bag at a slight angle.

YOU WILL NEED
Plain, shiny giftwrap
  or giftbag
Dried flowers and grasses
Ribbon
All-purpose glue
Scissors

POT-POURRI HEARTS

These delightful heart-shaped sachets are made from scraps of fabric and net. Fill the hearts with fragrant pot-pourri which can be bought from a chemist or beauty shop. The pot-pourri looks very pretty in the lacy hearts.

YOU WILL NEED
Lacy net fabric
Plain fabric
25cm (10in) narrow ribbon
10cm (4in) of 1.5cm (⅝in)
 wide ribbon
Pot-pourri
Needle and thread
Pinking shears
Pins and scissors
Tracing paper and pencil

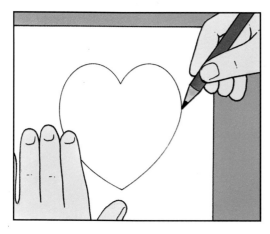

1 Using a pencil, trace the heart pattern on page 95. Cut out this pattern.

2 Pin the pattern on to both the lace and the fabric and carefully cut around the shape with pinking shears.

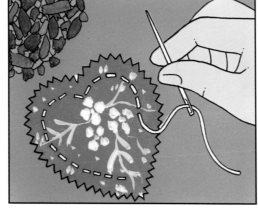

3 Sew together the lace and fabric hearts leaving a small gap at one edge. Pour some pot-pourri into the sachet and finish sewing around the heart. Make a hanging loop from the narrow ribbon and sew this to the top of the heart.

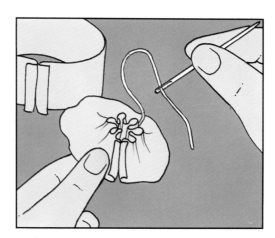

4 To make a little rosette, sew the ends of the length of wide ribbon together to make a circle. Sew a running stitch along one edge and gather up the thread tightly to form a little rosette. Sew the rosette to the front of the heart.

PRINTED EASTER EGGS

Use leaves, ferns or flowers to decorate eggs for Easter Day. The finished eggs can be placed in a large, attractive bowl, or threaded on to ribbon to make a pretty hanging decoration.

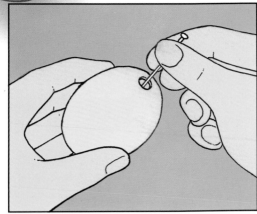

YOU WILL NEED

Eggs
Bowl
Needle
Fabric dye
Rubber gloves
Small ferns and leaves
Poster paints
Paintbrush

1 Gently scratch both ends of the egg with a needle to make a small hole. Make one hole 6mm (¼in) wide and the other 1cm (⅜in) wide.

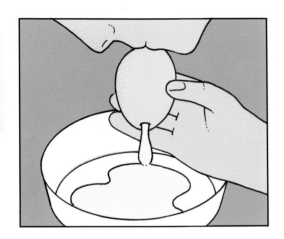

2 Poke the needle into the egg to break the yoke. Hold the egg over a bowl and blow gently through the small hole to empty the contents of the egg into the bowl.

3 Ask an adult to help you prepare the fabric dye following the instructions on the packet. Wearing rubber gloves, hold the egg in the dye solution for a few minutes, then take it out and leave it to dry.

4 Paint the ferns and leaves with poster paint and press them on to the egg, creating lovely patterns as you do so. Leave the eggs to dry thoroughly before using them.

SAFETY TIP: *Ask an adult to help you prepare the fabric dye.*

SHELL CREATURES

Create these cute little pets from shells you have collected on a beach holiday. Limpet shells make great tortoises, while smaller shells can be quickly turned into mice and snails.

YOU WILL NEED
Shells
Stick-on 'joggle' eyes
Embroidery thread
All-purpose glue

2 When you are happy with the animal shapes, stick the shells together with a strong, all-purpose glue.

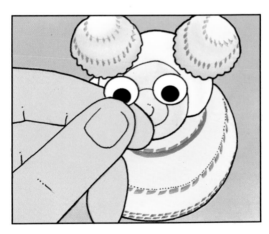

3 Glue on 'joggle' eyes where necessary. For example, tortoises and snails may not need eyes.

1 Hold the shells against one another to see which would make interesting creatures.

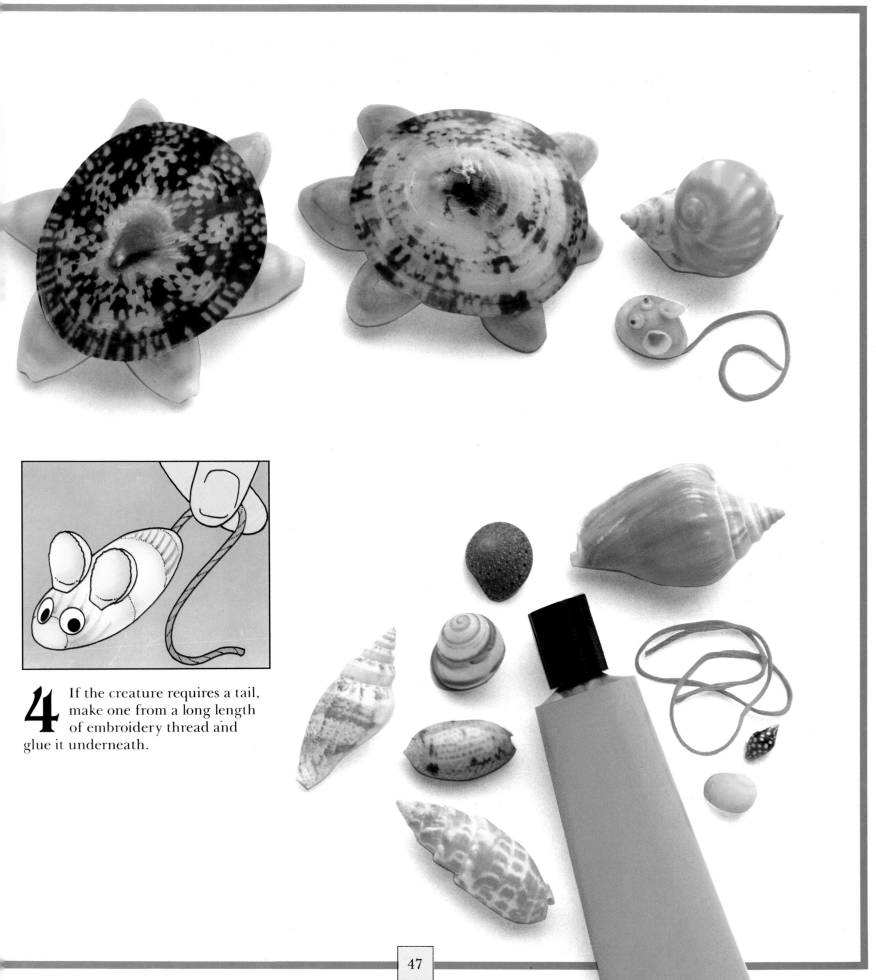

4 If the creature requires a tail, make one from a long length of embroidery thread and glue it underneath.

CORK COASTERS

Practical cork drinks coasters can be
transformed into a perfect gift idea by
adding some pretty dried strawflowers or
sunray daisies.

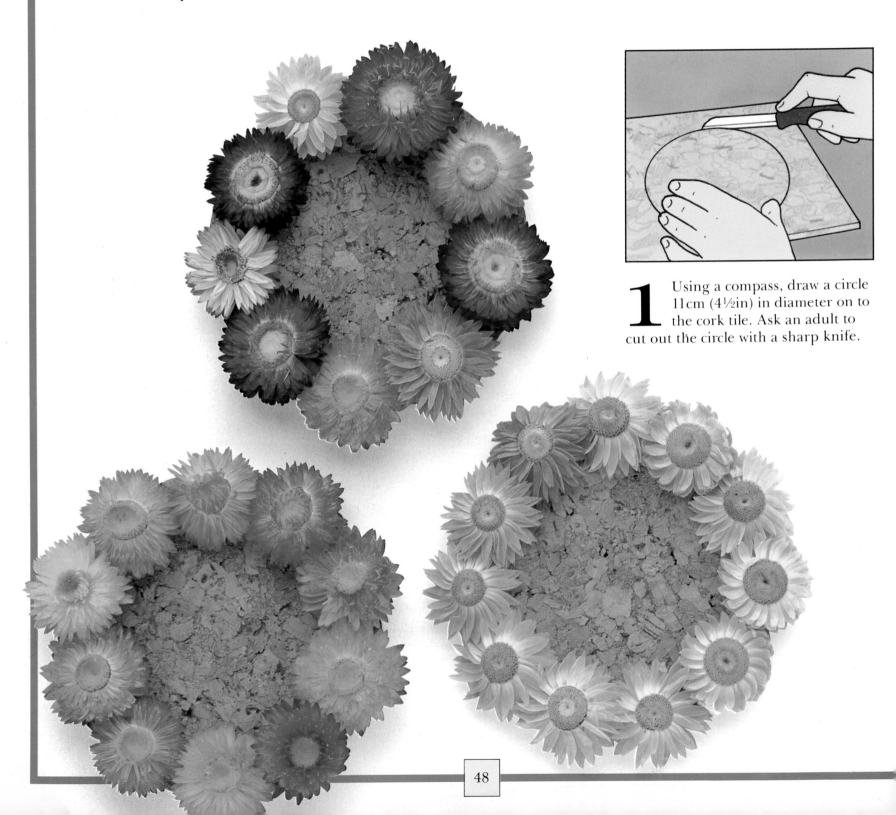

1 Using a compass, draw a circle
11cm (4½in) in diameter on to
the cork tile. Ask an adult to
cut out the circle with a sharp knife.

Glue the flower heads securely in position. Allow the glue to dry before using the coasters.

3 Arrange the flower heads in a ring around the edge of the cork coaster.

2 Using scissors, cut off the stems of the dried flowers close to the heads.

YOU WILL NEED
Dried flowers
Cork tile
All-purpose glue
Sharp knife
Compass and pencil
Scissors

SAFETY TIP: *Make sure an adult helps you when using a sharp knife.*

DRIED FLOWER POSY

A selection of dried flowers tied together with a brightly-coloured ribbon makes a perfect birthday present. Make the posy extra special by adding a lace doily.

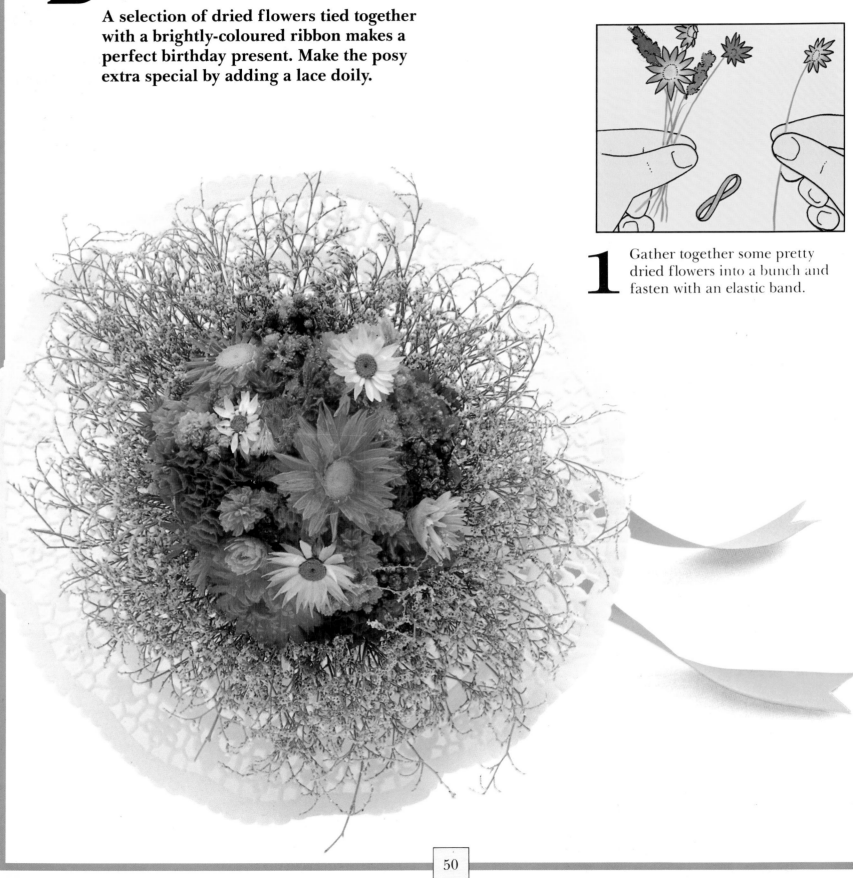

1 Gather together some pretty dried flowers into a bunch and fasten with an elastic band.

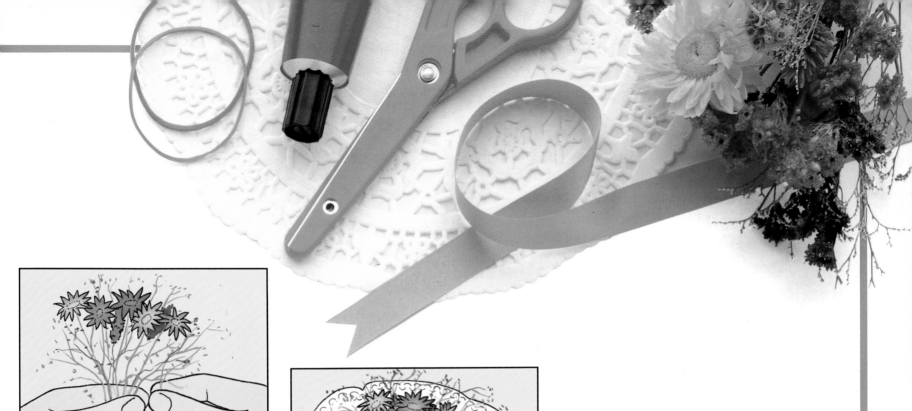

2 Position sprigs of sea lavender around the bunch and fasten the whole posy together with the other elastic band.

3 Cut a hole in the centre of a doily. Push the stems of the posy through the hole.

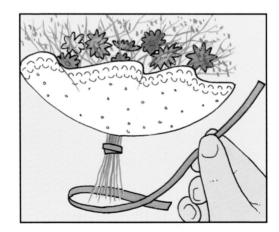

4 Dab a little glue to stick the doily to the stems of the posy. Tie a ribbon around the posy and finish with a pretty bow.

YOU WILL NEED
Dried flowers and
    Sea lavender
Paper doily
Ribbon
2 elastic bands
All-purpose glue
Scissors

51

KNOT GARDENS

In Elizabethan England, wealthy people would plant their herbs in strict geometric patterns. These were called knot gardens. Instead of herbs, you can create your own knot garden collage using natural materials such as beans, peas and lentils.

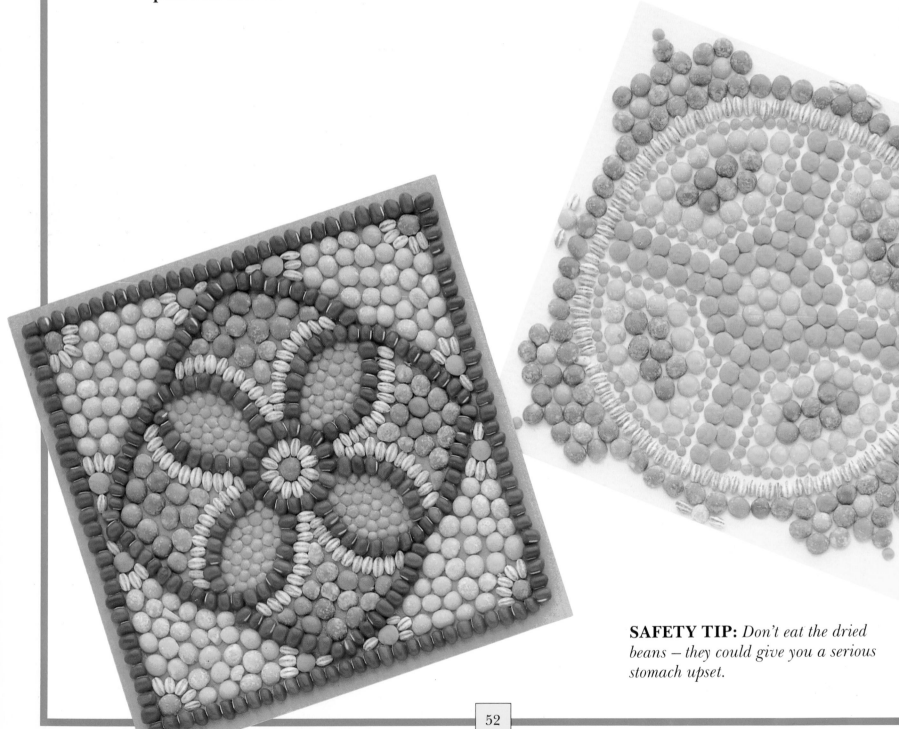

SAFETY TIP: *Don't eat the dried beans – they could give you a serious stomach upset.*

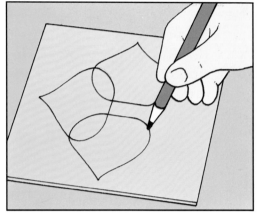

2 With a pencil, lightly draw a geometric pattern on to the card. If you prefer, copy the designs shown here.

3 Starting at the centre of the pattern, spread a little glue on to the card and press some of the pieces in position.

4 Continue working outwards, spreading the glue on in sections, until you have completely filled in the design.

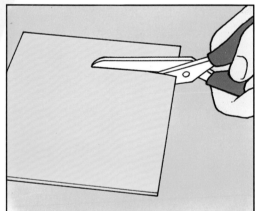

1 Using scissors, cut out a rectangle of firm card 15cm x 15cm (6in x 6in).

SHELL BOXES

Shells gathered from the beach can be used to decorate many things. Here, they adorn the top of a plain wooden box, turning it into a pretty jewellery casket.

YOU WILL NEED

Shells
Wooden box
Poster Paints
Paintbrush
All-purpose glue

1 Mix together the paint and water to make a thin, runny solution. Paint the box and leave it to dry.

2 Arrange the shells in a pretty pattern on the box lid. Position the largest shells first.

3 When you are happy with your design, carefully glue the shells in place.

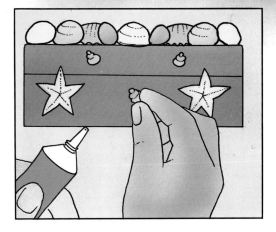

4 Leave the sides of the box plain or glue on a few small shells at random.

GOLDEN GIFTWRAP

Christmas giftwrap can be expensive to buy. This year wrap your presents in brown paper, but add a pretty arrangement of natural items such as cones and leaves, and a touch of gold paint.

1 Neatly wrap a present with brown parcel paper in the usual way.

4 You can also add loops or bows of giftwrap ribbon and glue them among the trimmings.

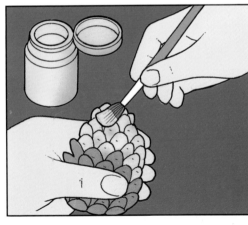

3 Paint some of the cones and other items with gold paint. Leave to dry. Arrange the different pieces on the gift and glue in place.

2 To make a gold-trimmed gift, tie gold giftwrap ribbon around the parcel, as shown.

YOU WILL NEED
Brown parcel paper
Scissors
Gold giftwrap ribbon
Fir cones
Seed pods
Dried leaves and grasses
Teasels
Cinnamon sticks
Tree bark
Gold poster paint
Paintbrush
All-purpose glue

DRIED FLOWER JEWELLERY

Make this pretty collection of summer jewellery using a selection of colourful dried flowers. Make a matching set of hair and fashion accessories or create your own designs to match your outfits.

1 To protect the most delicate dried flowers, paint them with a layer of craft varnish.

3 Arrange a pretty selection of dried flowers on to the brooch backs and the hair combs.

2 For the earrings, glue a single flower to the earring backs. Leave to dry in a safe place.

4 When you are happy with your design glue the flowers securely in position.

YOU WILL NEED

Dried flowers
Clip-on earring backs
Brooch backs
Hair combs
Hair slides
All-purpose glue
Craft varnish

FRUITY POTATO PRINTS

Potato prints can produce very professional results. Use them to print notepaper, gift tags and envelopes. Wash and re-use the same potato for a different colour, or make up several shapes on a few potatoes.

YOU WILL NEED
Washed potatoes
Poster paints
Paintbrush
Coloured writing paper
Ribbon
Sharp knife
Felt-tip pen
Hole punch

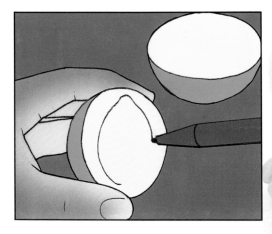

1 Using a sharp knife, cut a potato in half. Draw the fruit on one half with a felt-tip pen.

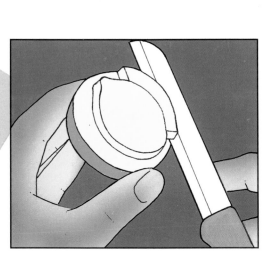

2 Holding the knife upright, cut around the outline of the fruit you have drawn, then cut away the potato around the fruit, leaving a raised, flat shape.

3 Using a paintbrush, apply a fairly thick layer of paint to the raised fruit shape, then press it firmly on to the paper.

4 You can print a motif at the top of a sheet of writing paper or fold the paper in half to make a notelet and print on to it a group of fruits.

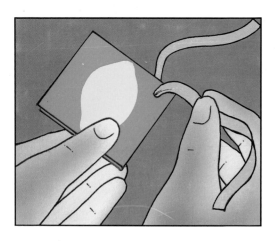

5 To make gift tags, cut a rectangle of paper and fold it in half. Punch a hole at the top of the tag and thread with ribbon.

SAFETY TIP: *Make sure an adult helps you when using a sharp knife.*

POT-POURRI BASKETS

These pretty little baskets make ideal gifts when filled with pot-pourri, especially when you have made your own mixture. Gather together dried flower heads, spices, leaves and petals, and add a few drops of essential oil to enhance the natural smell of the ingredients.

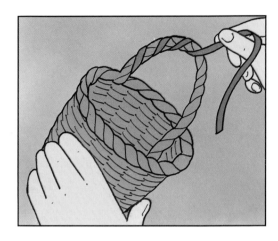

1 Wrap ribbon round the handle of the basket and weave some more through the rim if the basket weave is fairly open.

2 Make the pot-pourri from petals and flowerheads, bay leaves, spices – like crushed cinnamon sticks – and a few drops of essential oil; rose, sandalwood or lavender smell wonderful.

YOU WILL NEED
Small basket
Ribbon
Dried flowers
Petals, flowerheads,
  bay leaves,
  cinnamon sticks
Essential oil

3 Fill the baskets with two or three handfuls of the pot-pourri mixture.

4 Take miniature posies of dried flowers and tie them to the handle of the basket with ribbon bows.

FLOWER PAPERWEIGHTS

No one will believe you have made these wonderful paperweights. Although you have to buy the glass and varnish from specialist shops, you can pick and press your own flowers following the instructions given for Pressed Flower Cards on page 12.

1 Pour a little varnish into the recess of the paperweight. Move the base from side to side to spread the varnish evenly.

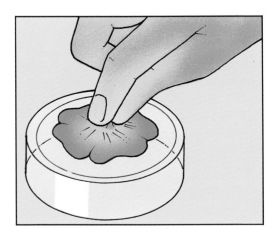

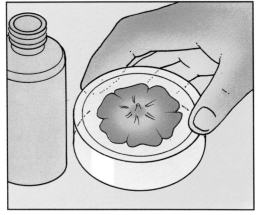

2 Carefully place a pressed flower face down on to the varnish. Pour a little more varnish over the top of the flower to cover it.

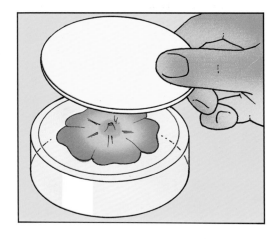

3 Move the paperweight again from side to side to spread the varnish. Leave the varnish to set hard for four to five days.

4 Cut a piece of card to fit in the recess of the paperweight. Finish the paperweight by covering the base with sticky-backed felt.

YOU WILL NEED
Glass paperweight with recessed base (from craft shops)
Pressed flowers
Craft varnish – Barbola is best (from craft shops)
Card and scissors
Sticky-backed felt

SEED JEWELLERY

Seeds collected from pumpkins and melons can be used to make fabulous modern jewellery. Colour the seeds with felt-tip pens and thread them on to elastic to make colourful bracelets and necklaces.

1 Leave the seeds to dry out overnight then carefully make a hole through each one with a large needle.

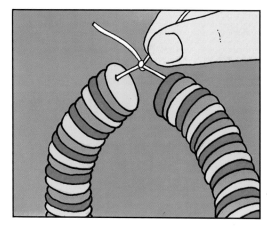

4 Fasten the ends of the elastic together with a tight knot. Shuffle the seeds along the elastic to hide the knot.

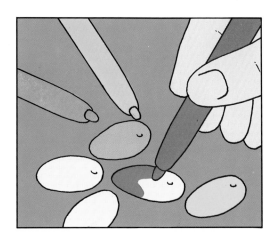

2 Colour one side of the seeds with felt-tip pens. Leave the seeds to dry, then colour the other sides too.

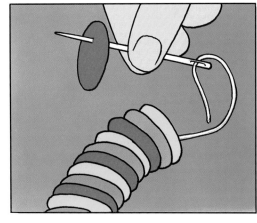

3 Thread the seeds on to the elastic until the string is long enough for a necklace, bracelet or pony-tail band.

YOU WILL NEED
Pumpkin or melon seeds
Waterproof felt-tip pens
Large needle
Hat elastic

STRING COLLAGE

This stylish box would make a perfect container for your jewellery. The string can be glued on in any design you like, but it is best to keep the shapes simple.

YOU WILL NEED
Wooden box
Pencil
Oddments of string
Poster paints
Paintbrush
All-purpose glue

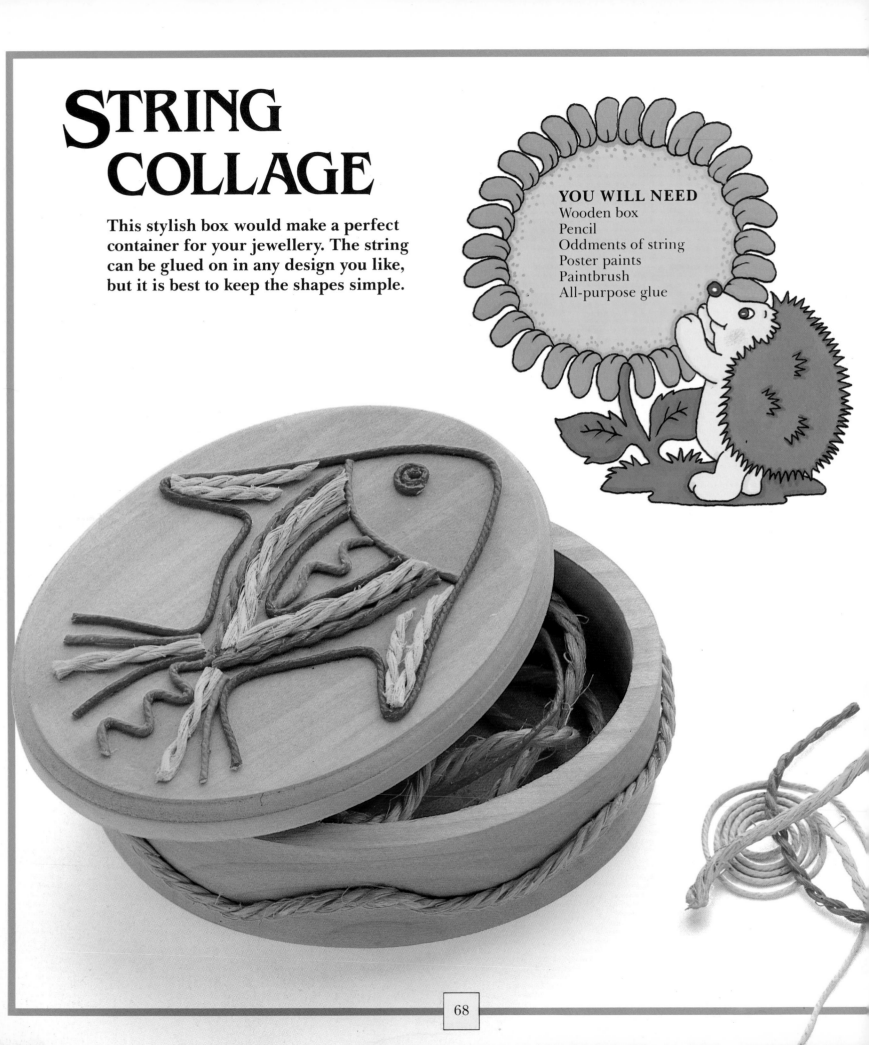

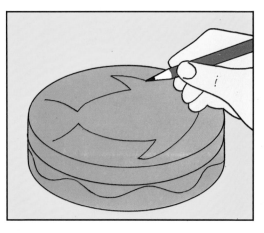

2 Using a pencil, lightly draw a simple fish shape on the lid and a wiggly line around the side of the box.

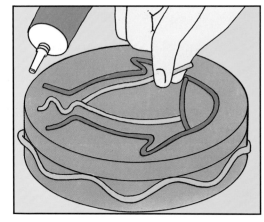

4 Fill in the fish with straight and wiggly lines of string. Glue in place on the box. Coil narrow string tightly to make an eye and glue to the fish.

1 Mix together a thin solution of paint and water. Paint the box and leave it to dry.

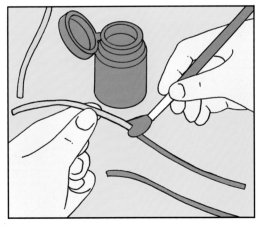

3 Paint the string with undiluted poster paints and leave to dry. Spread glue along the pencil lines, press a length of string on top.

BLOOMING BOOKMARKS

Pressing flowers and leaves is great fun and you can use them to make all sorts of original decorations and gifts, such as these pretty bookmarks. Always use freshly picked flowers and choose ones that are fairly flat as they are much easier to press.

YOU WILL NEED
Blotting paper
Heavy book
Flowers and leaves
Tweezers and card
Clear sticky-backed plastic
Ruler and ribbon
All-purpose glue
Scissors

1 Lay a sheet of blotting paper inside a large heavy book. Arrange small leaves and brightly-coloured flowers on to the blotting paper.

2 Place a second sheet of blotting paper over the flowers and leaves. Close the book and leave in a safe place.

3 After a few weeks, open the book and remove the flowers with tweezers. Arrange the flowers and leaves on to strips of card. When you are happy with the pattern, glue the flowers and leaves into place.

4 To protect the flowers, carefully cover the bookmarks with clear sticky-backed plastic film. Use a ruler to smooth out any air bubbles. Trim the edges with scissors and glue on a small ribbon bow.

JACK-O'-LANTERN

No Halloween would be complete without a traditional Jack-O'-Lantern to frighten away the spooks. Put a night light inside and place your finished lantern on a window sill.

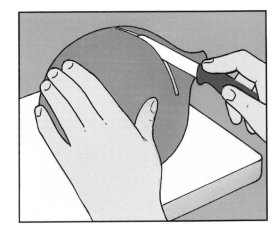

1 Using a sharp knife, slice the top off the swede or pumpkin. Ask an adult to help you do this.

SAFETY TIP: *Make sure an adult helps you when using a sharp knife.*

2 Cut out the inside of the swede or pumpkin with a knife. Ask an adult to do this for you. Draw a face on the front of the vegetable with a felt-tip pen.

3 Carefully cut around the outlines on the face with a sharp knife, then push out the features from the inside.

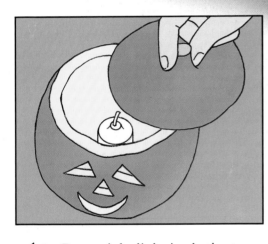

4 Put a night light in the lantern. Ask an adult to help you light it. Put the lid on top but do not leave the lit lantern unattended.

YOU WILL NEED
Swede or pumpkin
Sharp knife
Felt-tip pen
Night light

HERBY BATH FRAGRANCES

Hang these pretty herb sachets on to the bath tap. As the water runs through the bag, the herb fragrances will be carried into the water. Use any of the herb mixtures suggested here, or make up your own combinations.

1 From the muslin, cut an 18cm (7in) diameter circle. Place any of the herb mixtures in the centre of the circle.

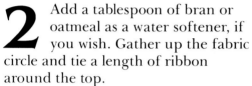

3 Tie the ribbon ends together in a bow so the bag can be hung on to a tap.

4 To finish, tuck some sprigs of herbs or lavender flowers under the ribbon.

2 Add a tablespoon of bran or oatmeal as a water softener, if you wish. Gather up the fabric circle and tie a length of ribbon around the top.

YOU WILL NEED
Dyed or natural muslin
Narrow ribbon
Scissors
Bran or oatmeal

For the herb mixtures:
Thyme and lavender
Lemon balm and rosemary
Camomile flowers
Apple mint and parsley
Sage and strawberry
   leaves

CHRISTMAS POMANDERS

These sweet-smelling pomanders are simple to make and look very festive tied up with brightly-coloured velvet ribbon. Make your own pot-pourri from dried flower heads and scented oils, or buy some already prepared.

YOU WILL NEED
Thick paintbrush
PVA glue
Ball of floral foam
Chunky pot-pourri
Velvet ribbon
All-purpose glue
Needle and thread

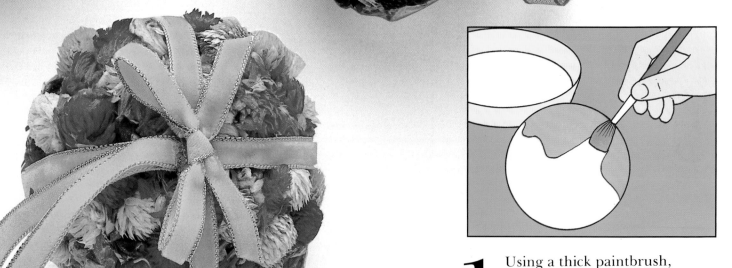

1 Using a thick paintbrush, spread PVA glue over a ball of floral foam. Press chunky pot-pourri into the ball while the glue is still wet.

2 Make sure the ball is completely covered with potpourri before leaving it to dry overnight in a safe place.

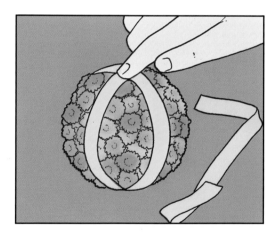

3 Cut two lengths of ribbon long enough to go round the pomander. Glue them in place.

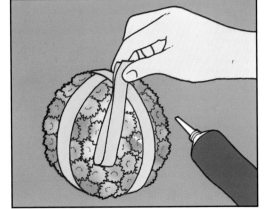

4 Make a small ribbon loop and glue or sew this to the top of the pomander so you can hang it up.

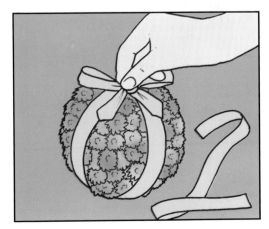

5 For a finishing touch, make a ribbon bow and glue this to the top of the pomander.

GOLDEN TREE DECORATIONS

These elegant, golden Christmas tree decorations have been made from pine cones and ivy leaves which you can collect on a country walk or even from your own garden.

1 Using a paintbrush, paint the cones and ivy leaves with gold paint. Thin the gold paint with a little water to get a good even colour.

2 To make the cone decoration, cut a length of ribbon and make a big bow. Glue this to the base of the cone, as shown.

3 To make the ivy decoration, take two ivy leaves and glue them on to another length of ribbon, sticking them a little distance apart. Make two bows using wider ribbon and glue these into position between the ivy leaves.

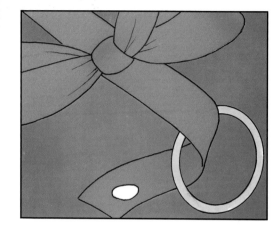

4 Thread the top of the ribbon through a curtain ring. Glue the end of the ribbon firmly in place behind the top bow.

YOU WILL NEED
Pine cones
Ivy leaves
Gold acrylic paint
Paintbrush
All-purpose glue
Curtain rings
Ribbon in
  two widths

WINTER SKIERS

Made from fir cones, these delightful little skiers can decorate a cake, the Christmas table or ski down the branches of your Christmas tree. The materials here make one skier.

YOU WILL NEED
A fir cone
2 wooden cocktail sticks
3.5cm (1¼in) cotton ball (from craft shops)
Cup of black tea
A clove
Felt scraps
Felt-tip pens
Acrylic paints and paintbrush
Coloured card and scissors
All-purpose glue
2 pipe cleaners

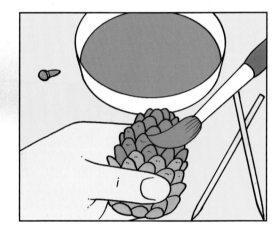

1 Paint the fir cone, clove and cocktail sticks with acrylic paint. Colour the cotton ball using a brush dipped in black tea. When dry, glue the cotton ball on to the fir cone.

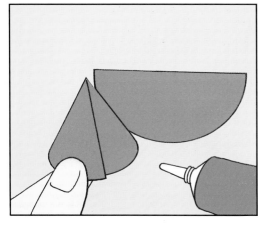

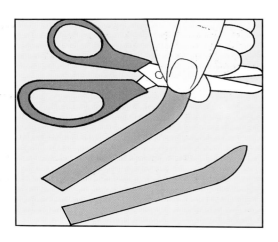

3 To make the hat, cut a circle from felt 10cm (4in) in diameter. Cut in half. Glue this into a cone shape and glue it on to the head.

4 Cut two pointed card strips for skis. Pull the points up between your finger and thumb to curve them upwards. Glue them underneath the fir cone.

2 Push the clove into the cotton ball as a nose. Draw on eyes and a mouth with felt-tip pens. For the scarf, cut a felt strip and snip a fringe into the ends. Tie around the neck.

5 For the arms, cut two pipe cleaners into 14cm (5½in) lengths, twist them together and wrap them around the cone. Bend the ends of the pipe cleaners around the cocktail sticks.

CHRISTMAS RAFFIA WREATH

Natural raffia and flowers make a beautiful wreath which you could hang up at any time of year. But with the addition of shiny ribbon and baubles, you can create the perfect decoration for Christmas time.

YOU WILL NEED
Natural raffia
5 small red baubles
Narrow red giftwrap ribbon
Red and pink dried flowers
Masking tape
All-purpose glue
Scissors

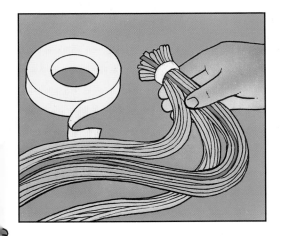

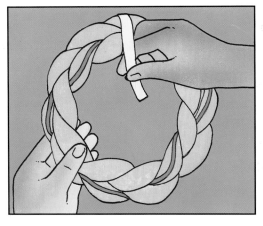

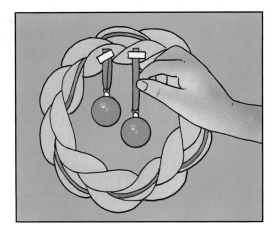

1 Cut three bundles of natural raffia 50cm (20in) long and one 50cm (20in) length of giftwrap ribbon. Bind the bundles of raffia and the ribbon together at one end with masking tape.

2 Plait the raffia and giftwrap ribbon and when complete overlap the ends to form a circle. Bind the ends together with masking tape.

3 Thread three of the baubles on to lengths of ribbon and hang them inside the wreath with masking tape. Glue flower heads to the top of the baubles.

4 Choose some long, trailing dried flowers and glue them either side of the wreath at the top. Glue a few flower heads and the other two baubles at the top of the wreath to hide the masking tape.

STRAW ANGELS

Made from completely natural materials, these straw angels will look great hanging from your Christmas tree this year. Give each angel a tiny posy of dried flowers or a handful of cones to hold.

1 Cut the heads from a bunch of dried barley. Strip off the leaves and soften the stems in warm water for two hours.

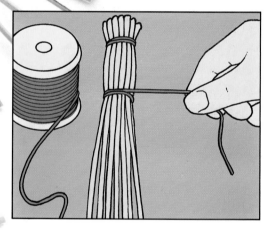

2 Cut 12 stems 18cm (7in) long. Hold the stems together and tie red thread around one end, and again 2.5cm (1in) away to make the head.

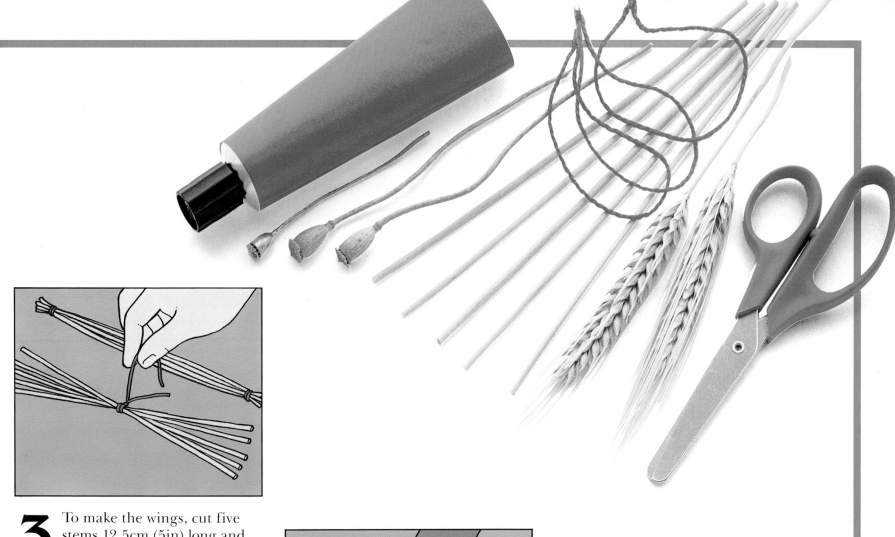

3 To make the wings, cut five stems 12.5cm (5in) long and bind them together in the middle. For the arms cut three stems 12.5cm (5in) long and bind them together at each end with red thread.

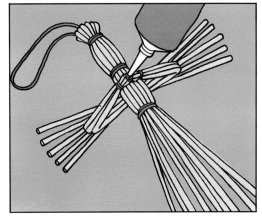

5 Bend the arms together in front and glue the hands together. To finish, make a loop from thread and glue it to the back of the head.

4 Slip the arms and wings between the long stems of the angel's body and bind directly beneath to make the waist.

YOU WILL NEED
Dried barley or wheat
Red embroidery thread
or wool
All-purpose glue
Dried flowers
Pine cones
Scissors

SANTA AND HIS HELPERS

Make a group of jolly Christmas characters from salt-dough – just flour, salt and water mixed together to form a dough. Paint them in bright, cheerful colours and hang them from the Christmas tree.

YOU WILL NEED
2 cups plain flour
1 cup salt
1 cup water
Gingerbread man pastry cutter
Poster paints
Craft varnish
Narrow ribbon
Blunt knife
Rolling pin
Pencil

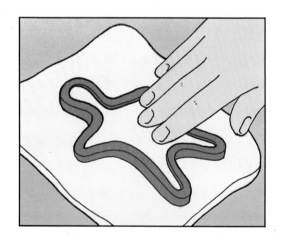

1 Mix the flour, salt and water together to make a firm dough. Roll out to 1cm (⅜in) thick and cut out the characters with a pastry cutter.

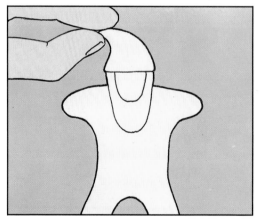

2 Mould a triangle for the beard and hat, flatten and press these to the head. Bend over the tip of the hat for the elves.

3 Cut out strips of dough for the belt, the cuffs on the sleeves and Santa's fur trim. Roll two balls of dough for the shoes and two small balls for the buttons. Now roll out small pieces of dough to make the eyes and nose. Press all the pieces into place. Make a hole in the tip of the hat to thread the ribbon through later.

4 Draw a smile on to the beard with the point of the pencil. Make little marks on Santa's fur trim and each of the beards using a blunt knife.

5 Ask an adult to help you bake the models in an oven for about 4 hours at 110°C/ 250°F/Gas mark ½. When the models are cool paint them in bright colours. Leave to dry before varnishing. Hang each one to the tree with ribbon.

SAFETY TIP: *Make sure an adult helps you when using the oven.*

CHRISTMAS LOG

This Christmas, make a bright and cheery table centrepiece from leaves and bark collected on a forest walk. Make sure that the bark is quite dry before using it.

1 With a blunt knife, cut a slice of floral foam about 6cm (2½in) thick. Glue the foam on top of the bark and when dry, slice away the corners, as shown.

2 Dampen the foam and push a candle holder into it. Put the candle into the holder.

3 Insert sprigs of holly, some with berries, into the foam around the candle holder.

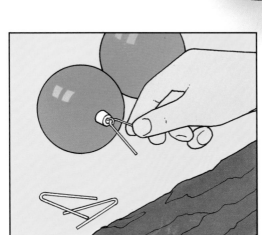

4 Bend a length of wire in half and push it through the hanging loop of the bauble. Tuck the baubles in among the sprigs of holly.

YOU WILL NEED
Tree bark
Floral foam
Candle holder
Red candle
Sprigs of holly
Green baubles
Floral wire
All-purpose glue
Blunt knife

RAFFIA NAPKIN RINGS

These brightly-coloured napkin rings are made from cardboard and natural raffia. The finished rings are stunning and no one would realize that you hadn't bought them from a highly-fashionable store.

YOU WILL NEED
Natural raffia
Fabric dye
Cardboard tube
All-purpose glue
Scissors

SAFETY TIP: *Ask an adult to help you prepare the fabric dye.*

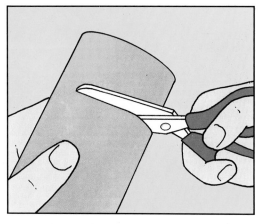

2 Remove the raffia, rinse it well and leave it to dry. Cut a cardboard tube into 3.5cm (1½in) lengths.

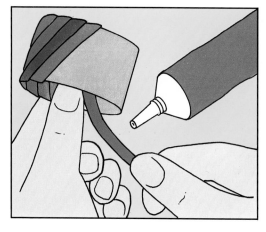

3 Bind one of the cardboard rings diagonally with the coloured raffia, glueing the ends securely inside.

1 Ask an adult to help you prepare the fabric dye following the instructions on the packet. Hold lengths of raffia in the dye for a few minutes.

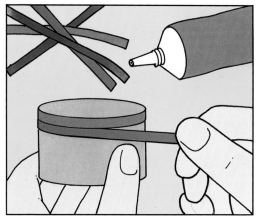

4 Another way to decorate a ring is to wind the raffia around it horizontally. Glue the ends inside the ring.

PATTERNS

The following pages show the patterns you will need to make some of the projects in the book. To find out how to copy a pattern follow the step-by-step instructions given for each project.

   You may want to make a pattern that you can keep to use again. To do this trace over the outline of the pattern with a pencil. Turn your tracing over and lay it on to a piece of thick card. Rub firmly over the outline with a pencil. The image will appear on the card. Cut out the shape. If you keep this pattern in a safe place, you can use it time and time again.

COCKATIEL COLLAGE

Page **14**

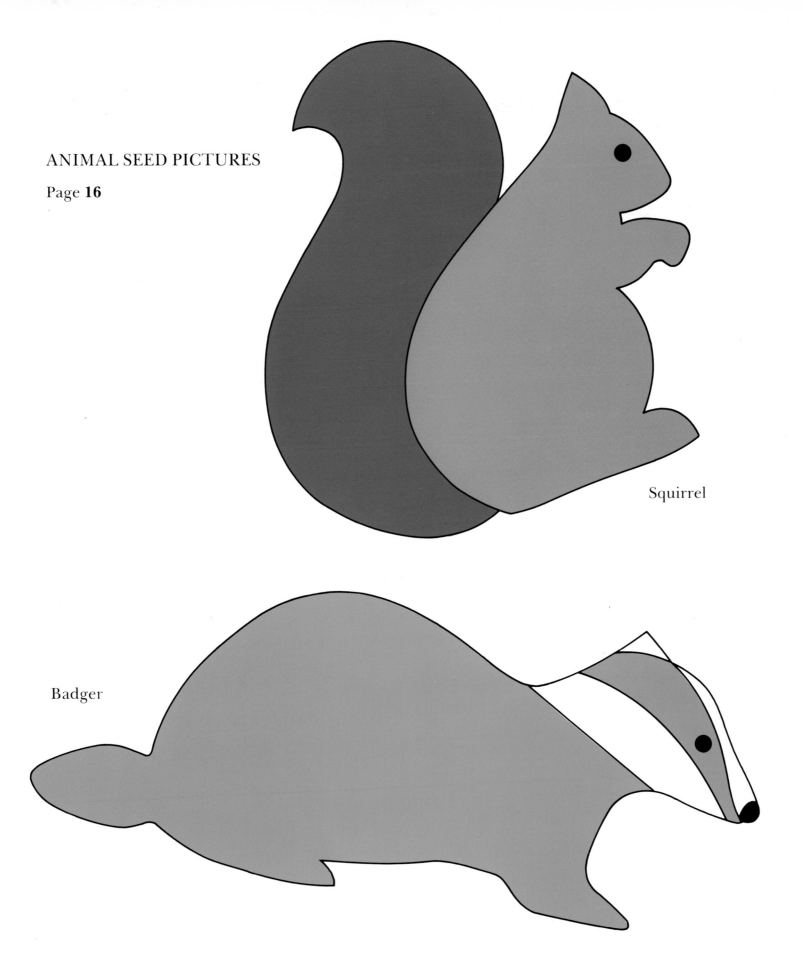

Squirrel

Badger

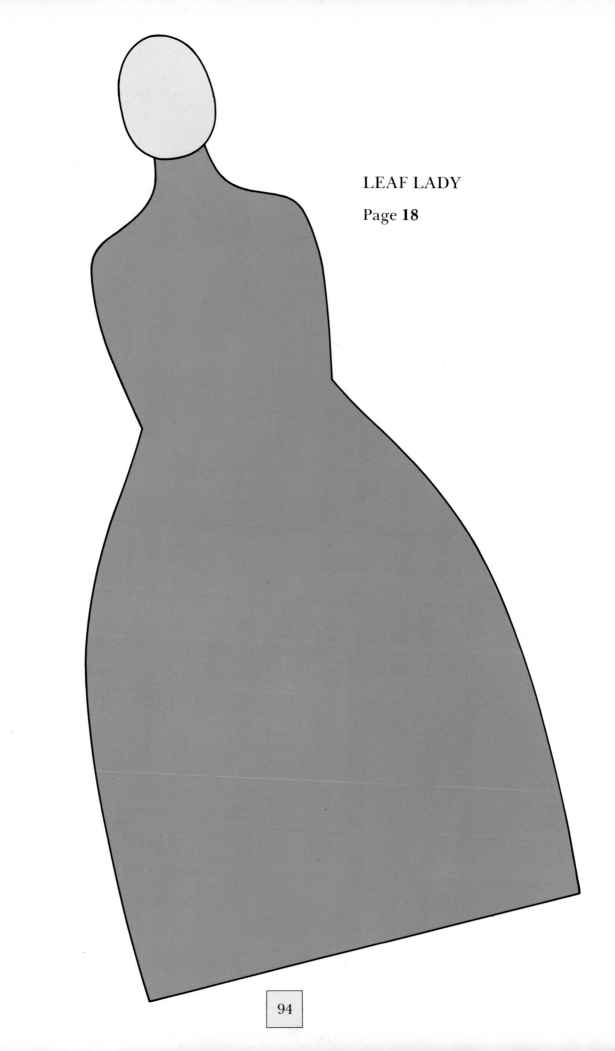

LEAF LADY

Page **18**

MRS TEASEL HEDGEHOG

Page **32**

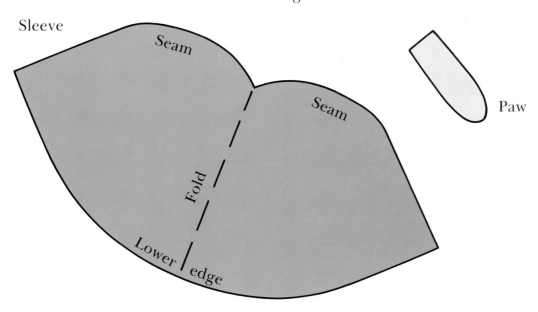

Sleeve

Seam

Seam

Fold

Lower edge

Paw

POT-POURRI HEARTS

Page **42**

INDEX